Introduction

The recipes I have selected for this, my first, b..... .. .
are traditional to the Punjab area of the Indian Sub-Continent. For many
years now my friends, neighbours and colleagues have asked me for
recipes after tasting different dishes I have produced. Over 500 copies of a
collation of recipes have already been sold for various charitable causes.
As a result of listening to users and buyers I have made my recipe book
very user friendly by including step by step illustrations for the more
complicated instructions. There is also a colour photograph of almost
every completed product and I have also included several recipes which
are much healthier than any that are sold commercially.

The amounts of spices I have indicated are a rough guide. If you wish,
start by adding less and adjust the quantities of spices to suit your own
palate by testing the food before it is completely cooked and add more if
required. My best advice is to make sure you always "balance" the salt
with the chillies. If the food catches the back of your throat then add a
little more salt.

All my recipes (except 1) serve 4-6 people. A selection of the starters
can be served as a main course. You can choose whether to eat your
main courses with rice, chuppattis, naans, pitta bread etc. Why not try
a different combination each time!

Please note that Healthy Options have been identified by ✱.
For healthier main courses reduce the amount of oil used.

I would like to take this opportunity to wish you every success in your
cooking and always remember that the second attempt is usually better
than the first and of course "practice makes perfect".

Tasnim

Contents

Gharam Masala

Chilli Powder

Salt

Tandoori Masala

Haldi

Mixed Whole Spices

Whole cardamom pods with Seeds removed from Shell

Whole Coriander Seeds

Ground Gharam Masala

Spices

Chilli powder
Use extra hot red chilli powder for all the recipes and adjust amount as desired. However, to retain the colour for a milder curry use a milder chilli powder.

Haldi
Haldi or turmeric is a bright yellow powder which enhances the colour of the curries and improves the flavour.

Tandoori Masala
Another blend of spices but this time it is red in colour and enhances the flavour of the chicken or meat.

Gharam Masala
This is a blend of lots of different spices eg black peppers, cloves, cinnamon etc. Gharam masala is brown in colour and is sold ready made but the best type is freshly made at home in small quantities. Take any quantity of mixed whole spices and an equal quantity of whole coriander seeds. Remove the outer shell of the large cardamom pods. Grind in a coffee grinder or spice mill until all the spices are fine. (Not advisable to use the same grinder for coffee and spices.) It can then be stored in a container with a tight lid for about 3 months.

Root Ginger

Garlic

Ginger &
Garlic Paste

Green chillies

Remove the stalks from 5oog of fresh green chillies and rinse using warm water. Do not remove the seeds. Place in a food processor and add a heaped teaspoon of salt. Using a chopping blade process until seeds are as fine as possible. Store the chopped chillies in a jar with a tight lid (an empty jam jar will do) and place in a freezer until required.
The "frozen" chillies can be used straight from the freezer.

Ginger & Garlic

Remove the outer layer from root ginger. Take an equal quantity of garlic and remove the outer layer. If a large quantity of garlic is being prepared at once then break the cloves into segments and soak in hot water. This makes it easier to remove the skin. Place equal quantities of ginger and garlic in a food processor and use a chopping blade process until a paste is formed. Keep a jar of paste in the fridge and place the rest in small jars and freeze.

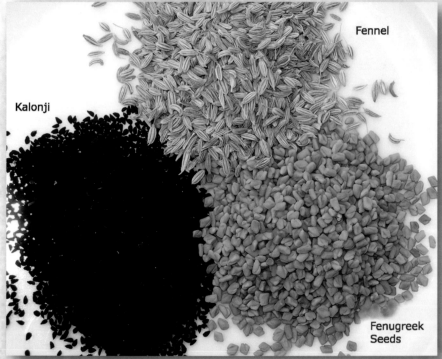

Fennel

Kalonji

Fenugreek
Seeds

Fresh coriander

If coriander stems are tender there is no need to remove leaves from the stem but simply chop off roots and roughly chop the remaining coriander. Store unwashed fresh coriander in a food bag or plastic container in a fridge for a few days and rinse with cold water before use. Wash the remaining chopped coriander with cold water and allow to drain.
Place in a freezer bag and use straight from the freezer when required.

Kalonji (black onion seed), Fenugreek seeds and Fennel:
spices used for specialised recipes.

Lamb Samosas

Filling

500g of minced lamb
500g of frozen garden peas
600g of onions *(finely chopped)*
500g of potatoes *(diced into small pieces approx 1cm cubes)*
1 heaped teaspoon of green chillies *(see page on spices)*
2 heaped teaspoons of salt
2 heaped teaspoons of gharam masala
1 heaped teaspoon red chilli powder
1 heaped teaspoon ginger/garlic paste *(see page on spices)*
1 handful of fresh coriander *(see page on spices)*

Pastry

500g of plain flour *(keep a couple of teaspoons for paste)*
2 tablespoons of sunflower oil

Method for Filling

Apart from the coriander, gharam masala and peas place all of the remaining ingredients in a strong saucepan or wok. Cook using a high temperature until all the liquid has boiled away.

Add peas and gharam masala and again cook until all excess water has boiled off.

While cooking stir regularly making sure that the mixture does not stick to the pan. Add the coriander and cook for another couple of minutes. Leave the mince mixture to cool. The filling can also be frozen for later use or kept in the fridge overnight to split the workload!

Flour & Water Paste

Samosas

Puff Pastry Rolls

Method for Pastry (See easier alternatives on next 2 pages)

Add oil to sifted flour. Add enough cold water a little at a time to make a firm dough.

Allow the dough to sit for about 10 minutes. Divide into small balls (about the size of a table-tennis ball). Press down on each ball to cover with dry flour on each side and then roll out into a round approx 8 inches or 20 cm in diameter. Heat lightly on a medium hot griddle, on both sides (or use a strong frying pan). When each round of pastry is cooked keep wrapped in a tea towel so that it does not dry out. The rounds can be placed on top of each other in the tea towel.

When all the rounds are made, cut in half to make semi-circles.
Fold each semi-circle one at a time into a cone shape. Stick edge with a paste made from plain flour and water. Fill cones with cold minced lamb filling and seal outer edge with flour paste. Using a fork press outer edge firmly to make sure the samosas are sealed completely.

Deep fry samosas in medium hot oil 4 or 5 at a time depending on size of fryer. Do not allow samosas to brown too quickly. Fry until golden brown - stir occasionally.

If you wish to freeze samosas do not fry them but leave uncooked samosas in fridge overnight and then place in freezer bags. Defrost completely before frying.

Mixed Vegetables

Diced Potatoes

Green Chillies

Chopped Onions

Vol-au-vents & Spring Rolls

Chicken Samosas

See Lamb Samosas but use minced chicken instead.

Vegetarian Samosas

See Lamb Samosas but omit the lamb and peas and use 1kg of frozen mixed vegetables instead.

Spring Rolls

Make filling as for lamb samosas or vegetable samosas.

Ready - made "Chinese pastry" sheets are available in Oriental food stores which make an easier alternative to samosa pastry. Follow instructions on the packet or my illustrations for rolling up spring rolls. Use the flour and water paste to stick the final edges. Fry as samosas.

Spring rolls can also be frozen *(see samosas)*.

Vol–au–Vents

Make filling as for lamb samosas or vegetable samosas (or use any left over filling).

Use ready made vol-au-vent cases and bake following the instructions on the packet. Fill each with filling of your choice.

Lamb Filling

Block of Puff Pastry

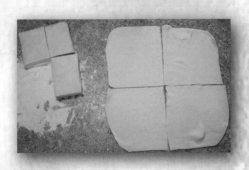

Puff Pastry Lattice

Puff Pastry Rolls

Make filling as for lamb samosas or vegetable samosas.

Defrost a block of frozen puff pastry. Cut into 4 equal pieces. Roll each piece into an 8 inch or 20 cm square. Cut each of the 20 cm squares into 4 pieces. Brush beaten egg round the edges of all 16 pieces of pastry (This part is optional as the egg just helps to seal the edges.)

Place a spoonful of filling in the middle of the small piece of puff pastry and fold pastry over like a sausage roll. Brush pastry rolls with beaten egg and bake in oven. *(See instructions on pastry for temperatures.)*

Frozen puff pastry is also available as a ready rolled sheet to make life easier!

Puff Pastry Lattice

Make filling as for lamb samosas or vegetable samosas.

Defrost a block of frozen puff pastry. Cut in half and roll each piece into a rectangle that fits on a baking tray. (I use a Swiss roll tray.) Cut equally spaced slits through the pastry on each side and place filling in the centre area. Cross each alternate slit into the middle creating a pleated effect. Brush the the top with beaten egg and bake in oven. *(See instructions on pastry for temperatures.)*

Chopped
Spinach

Diced
Potatoes

Chopped
Onions

Coriander

Chopped
Spring Onions

Vegetable Pakoras

300g of potatoes cut into small pieces
300g of onions finely chopped
3 spring onions finely chopped
6 spinach leaves finely chopped *(use frozen spinach leaves if fresh not available)*
1 heaped teaspoon of green chillies *(see page on spices)*
1 heaped teaspoon of salt
$^1/_2$ teaspoon of red chilli powder
1 teaspoon gharam masala
1 teaspoon tandoori masala *(optional but gives more colour)*
1 tablespoon of lemon juice
250g of gram flour *(chick pea flour)*
50g of self raising flour
Sunflower oil

Sift gram flour and self raising flour into a bowl and add all spices and the lemon juice. Add cold water a little at a time and mix to form a smooth paste. Set aside for approx 10 minutes (prepare vegetables while waiting.)

Add all remaining ingredients to the batter and mix thoroughly making sure all the vegetables are fully coated with batter. Pakora batter should drop off a spoon readily - add more water or gram flour to give desired consistency.

Drop a tablespoon of batter at a time in hot oil. Fill pan or wok with pakoras and deep fry until golden brown. (Oil is at right temperature if after a minute the pakoras rise to top of oil.) Stir occasionally while pakoras are frying. Each batch should take about 5 minutes.

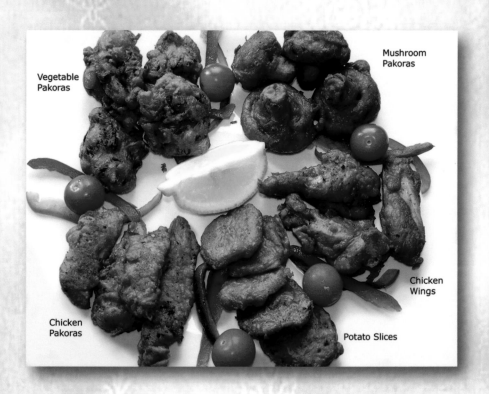

Vegetable Pakoras

Mushroom Pakoras

Chicken Pakoras

Potato Slices

Chicken Wings

Fish or Chicken Pakoras

Fish or chicken breast cut into slices.
1 heaped teaspoon of green chillies *(see page on spices)*
1 heaped teaspoon of salt
$1/2$ teaspoon of red chilli powder
1 teaspoon of gharam masala
1 teaspoon of tandoori masala
1 tablespoon of lemon juice
250g of gram flour *(chick pea flour)*
50g of self raising flour

Sift gram flour and self raising flour into a bowl and add all spices.
Add cold water a little at a time and mix to form a smooth paste.
Set aside for approx 10 minutes (prepare fish/chicken while waiting).

Add the fish/chicken slices to the batter making sure all the pieces of fish/chicken are fully coated with batter. Pakora batter should drop off a spoon readily - add more water to give desired consistency. Leave to marinate for as long as possible. (I usually leave overnight but this is not essential.)

Drop each piece of battered fish/chicken one at a time in medium hot oil. Fill pan with pakoras and deep fry until golden brown making sure the pakoras are cooked right through. (Oil is at right temperature if after a minute the pakoras rise to top of oil.) Stir occasionally while pakoras are frying. Each batch should take about 5 minutes.

Variations

Instead of fish or chicken breast use any vegetables of your choice e.g. courgettes, aubergines, mushrooms or thin slices of potato. Chicken wings are also great for frying in this same batter.

Aaloo Tikka

1 packet of potato mash
1 heaped tablespoon of gram flour *(sifted)*
1 heaped teaspoon of green chillies *(see spices page)*
$1/2$ heaped teaspoon of salt
1 heaped teaspoon of gharam masala
1 heaped teaspoon of tandoori masala
1 level teaspoon of red chilli powder
1 handful of fresh coriander *(see spices page)*
1 egg beaten

Place all ingredients except the egg in a bowl. Mix thoroughly. Form into flat rounds about 3 inches or 8cm in diameter and 0.5cm thick.

Coat in beaten egg and shallow fry, in medium hot oil, turning 2 or 3 times. Fry a few at a time for about 3-4 minutes. Drain and serve.

Aaloo Tikka Plus

Use the same ingredients as aaloo tikka and add a variety of other vegetables eg chopped spring onions or ordinary onions, slices of peppers or sweetcorn.

Tuna fish or salmon can also be added to the same ingredients but drain off all the oil or brine before adding to the rest of the ingredients.

Channa Chaatt Healthy Option as no extra fat is used

800g of boiled chick peas *(drain and wash with hot water)*
300g of sliced onions *(keep a few slices for decorating)*
300g of potatoes *(chopped into small pieces)*
1 heaped teaspoon of green chillies *(see spices page)*
1 heaped teaspoon of gharam masala
2 heaped teaspoons of salt
$1/2$ teaspoon red chilli powder
2 teaspoons of tamarind paste
1 handful of coriander leaves

Apart from the tamarind paste and the boiling water, place the rest of the ingredients in a strong saucepan and fry for approx 10 minutes on a medium heat making sure to stir regularly. Dissolve the tamarind paste in 800mls of boiling water and pour over the chick peas. Continue to simmer until most of the liquid has been absorbed (approx 20 minutes). Place in serving dish and allow the chaatt to cool. When ready to serve cover with fresh chopped coriander and a few slices of raw onion.

Chicken

Lamb
Chops

Seekh
Kebabs

Barbecued
Seekh
Kebabs

Barbecued
Chicken

Shaami Kebabs

250g of minced lamb
250g of yellow split peas *(wash and soak overnight)*
2 heaped teaspoons of green chillies *(see spices page)*
1 heaped teaspoon of gharam masala
1 level teaspoon of red chilli powder
1¹/2 teaspoons of salt
2 eggs separated

Place the drained yellow split peas and minced lamb in a strong saucepan and add enough water to cover the mixture. Simmer slowly until the yellow split peas are tender, adding more water if necessary. Allow to cool and then using a food processor process the mixture until quite fine. Add the remaining ingredients, binding together using the egg yolks. (Do not add the egg whites.)

Knead to form a smooth mixture. Form into flat rounds about 3 inches or 8 cm in diameter and 0.5 cm thick. Coat in egg white and shallow fry in medium hot oil turning 2 - 3 times. Fry a few at a time for about 3 - 4 minutes. Drain and serve.

Seekh Kebabs Healthy Option as only a little extra fat is used

500g of minced lamb
1 heaped teaspoon of green chillies *(see spices page)*
1 level teaspoon of red chilli powder
1 heaped teaspoon of gharam masala
1¹/2 teaspoons of salt
Olive oil or sunflower oil

Knead all ingredients to form a smooth mixture. Refrigerate for at least 2 hours. (I usually leave overnight.) Shape onto skewers.
Barbecue or grill on moderate heat for about 15 minutes brushing the kebabs lightly with olive oil or sunflower oil while being cooked.

Simple Kebabs Healthy Option as no extra fat is used

500g of minced lamb or minced chicken
300g onions finely chopped
1 egg
1 heaped teaspoon of green chillies *(see spices page)*
1 heaped teaspoon of gharam masala
1 heaped teaspoon of salt
1 level teaspoon of red chilli powder
1 handful of fresh coriander *(see spices page)*

Place all the ingredients in a bowl. Mix thoroughly. Divide into 12 and form
each into a burger. Place on a baking tray. (Line a tray with aluminium foil
to ease the washing up!) Cook in an oven for 15 minutes at 220ºC.
Place the kebabs on a grill pan and finish cooking them in a hot grill
by browning both sides.

Barbecue Chicken Healthy Option as only a little extra fat is used
(see page 33 for photograph)

4 chicken breasts cut into smaller pieces to go onto skewers
450g of natural yoghurt
1 heaped teaspoon of green chillies *(see spices page)*
1 heaped teaspoon of gharam masala
2 heaped teaspoons of tandoori masala
2 heaped teaspoons of salt
1 heaped teaspoon red chilli powder
1 tablespoon of lemon juice
Olive oil or sunflower oil

Mix all the other ingredients together and then coat the chicken pieces
with this marinade. Refrigerate overnight or for at least 2 hours. Place on
skewers and barbecue. Brush lightly with oil while cooking and serve
immediately.

Aachari Potatoes Healthy Option if you omit the oil

1 kg of baby potatoes *(or ordinary potatoes chopped into small pieces)*
150g of onions
400g of tinned tomatoes
1 heaped teaspoon of green chillies *(see spices page)*
1 level teaspoon of red chilli powder
1 heaped teaspoon of gharam masala
1 heaped teaspoon of kalonji *(black onion seed)*
1 heaped teaspoon of fenugreek seeds
1 heaped teaspoon of fennel
$1^1/_2$ teaspoons of salt
50ml of distilled malt vinegar
50ml of lemon juice
25 ml of olive oil or sunflower oil *(omit for a healthier option)*

Place roughly chopped onion, tomatoes and all the spices in a food processor and blend to form a paste. Pour into a bowl. Apart from the potatoes add the rest of the ingredients and mix thoroughly. Stir in the potatoes making sure they are coated in the marinade. Leave for at least 2 hours and then roast in a hot oven (260ºC) for approx 1 hour.
While roasting turn the potatoes in the marinade at least 2 times.
Adjust the temperature and cooking time accordingly to the type of potatoes you have used.

Aachari Chicken Wings

Tandoori Chicken Wings

Aachari Chicken

6 chicken wings *(cut into 12 pieces)* or 2 chicken breasts
30ml of olive oil
1 heaped teaspoon of ginger and garlic paste *(see spices page)*
1 heaped teaspoon of kalonji *(black onion seed)*
1 heaped teaspoon of fenugreek seeds
1 heaped teaspoon of fennel
1 level teaspoon of red chilli powder
1 heaped teaspoon of haldi
1 heaped teaspoon of salt
25ml of distilled malt vinegar
25ml of lemon juice

Place oil in a wok or non stick pan and add the ginger and garlic paste.
Fry using a moderate heat for a minute and then add the kalonji,
fenugreek seeds and fennel. Stir and fry for another minute before adding
the chilli powder and the haldi. Now add the chicken and continue frying
on a moderate heat for about 20 minutes. If the ingredients start to stick to
the wok then add a few drops of water and stir more regularly. Finally add
the vinegar and lemon juice and fry for a further 10 minutes. Serve the
chicken with any spices sticking to it but throw away the rest.

Marinated Chicken

Tandoori Chicken Healthy Option as no extra fat is used

1 chicken *(remove skin and joint into small pieces or use boneless whole chicken, chicken breast, drum sticks or thighs)*
450g of natural yoghurt
1 heaped teaspoon of green chillies *(see spices page)*
1 heaped teaspoon of gharam masala
2 heaped teaspoon of tandoori masala
2 heaped teaspoons of salt
1 heaped teaspoon of red chilli powder
1 tablespoon of lemon juice

Prepare chicken and set aside. Mix all the other ingredients together and then coat the chicken pieces with this marinade. Refrigerate overnight or for at least 2 hours. (The spices will soak into the chicken better if allowed to marinate for a longer period of time.) The marinated chicken can be frozen and defrosted completely before cooking.

Line a roasting tin with aluminium foil and place the chicken and all of the marinade into the roasting tray. Cover the chicken with more foil and seal the edges by folding the 2 layers together round the outside.

Place in a hot oven (240ºC) for approximately 1 hour or until chicken is cooked (turn chicken at least once during roasting). Remove the top foil cover for the last 10 minutes of roasting.

If you wish to make this into a main meal then place some onion slices in with the chicken. Serve with aachari potatoes, sweetcorn and garlic bread. Or slice some carrots, dice some potatoes and pour a little sunflower over the vegetables. Sprinkle with mixed herbs and bake in the same oven as the chicken.

Tandoori Lamb Chops
Healthy Option as no extra fat is used

1kg of lamb chops
450g of natural yoghurt
1 heaped teaspoon of green chillies *(see spices page)*
1 heaped teaspoon of gharam masala
1 heaped teaspoon of tandoori masala
1 heaped teaspoon of salt
1 heaped teaspoon of red chilli powder
2 tablespoons of lemon juice

Make marinade by mixing all the ingredients together and then make sure all the chops are coated in the marinade. Use lamb chops or chunks of lamb if you do not like eating off the bone! Lamb should be marinated overnight or even for two days and kept refrigerated. The marinated lamb can also be frozen and defrosted completely before being cooked.

Tandoori lamb is best cooked in a grill or on the barbecue. Grill the chops or lamb pieces in a hot grill turning 2 or 3 times. For well done chops cook for approximately 25 minutes under an electric grill.

Browned Onions

Chicken In Fried Onions Just Before Adding The Rice

Chicken Pilau Rice

2 chicken breasts (cut into bite size pieces)
150g of onions (finely chopped)
400g of basmati rice (Wash until water runs clear and then cover with water and leave to soak for about 30 minutes).
2 heaped teaspoons of gharam masala
2 heaped teaspoons of salt
1 heaped teaspoon of ginger and garlic paste
1/4 teaspoon of red chilli powder
20ml of olive oil or sunflower oil

Place onions, oil and salt in a strong saucepan and fry using a high heat until onions are soft. Make sure the onions do not stick to the pan (stir frequently using a wooden spatula and add a few drops of water if necessary). Add the chilli powder and the gharam masala and continue frying until onions are quite brown. Add the chicken pieces and fry until chicken is cooked (approx 10 minutes).

Drain the soaked rice and add to the chicken. Immediately add 900ml of boiling water. Using the highest temperature allow the rice to soak up the boiled water. Stir carefully 2 or 3 times making sure not to break the rice.

When only a thin film of water remains turn the heat down to as low as possible (this should only take about 5 minutes). Wrap a tea-towel round the lid of the saucepan and place on pot. (This will soak up any excess water.) Leave the heat low and allow to "simmer" for about 10 minutes.

Gently turn rice in pot before serving taking care not to break the rice.

Lamb Pilau Rice

Use lamb pieces instead of chicken.
See chicken pilau rice for remaining ingredients.

Fry onions with all of the spices for about 5 minutes and then add lamb pieces. When half cooked (approx 15 minutes) add 300mls of water and fry until lamb is tender. Continue as for chicken pilau rice.

Vegetable Pilau Rice

Instead of chicken or lamb use approximately 500g of frozen peas, chick peas, potatoes or frozen mixed vegetables. (Or a combination of these) If using dried chick peas they must be soaked overnight and then boiled for about 30 minutes until soft. (Or use a tin of boiled chick peas but wash in hot water first as they are usually soaked in brine.)

Brown onion as for chicken pilau rice and then add the vegetables of your choice. Continue as for chicken pilau rice.

Chopped Onions

Red Chilli Powder

Haldi

Ginger & Garlic Paste

Gharam Masala

Salt

Onion Sauce Ready to Store

Onion Sauce Ready to Use

Useful Hints

The basis of most of my curries is the onion sauce described below. If you like a thick sauce, then add more onions and fewer onions for a thinner sauce. Adjust quantities of red chilli powder and salt to suit your own taste.

I usually make a large batch of the sauce ready to use and store in the fridge or freezer. To do this do not add the chilli powder or haldi and only use a quarter of the oil. These can be added at the time of cooking and the required amounts can be used. Empty 1kg margarine tubs are great containers for storing one portion of onion sauce and once it is cold, it can then be kept in the fridge for up to a week or in the freezer for several weeks. I strongly recommend making up batches of onion sauce so that your cooking and preparation time will be greatly reduced.

Onion Sauce (1 Portion)

1 kg of onions *(finely chopped)*
200g tin of tomatoes
50ml of olive oil or sunflower oil
1 heaped teaspoon of ginger and garlic paste
1 to 2 heaped teaspoons of salt
1 to 2 heaped teaspoons of red chilli powder
$1/4$ teaspoon of haldi

If a food processor is available then chop onions roughly and place in processor with the tomatoes and use chopping blade to process until quite pureed. (Otherwise chop onions by hand.)

Place the onions, tomatoes, ginger and garlic paste, salt and oil in a strong saucepan and fry until onions are soft and the oil separates out. Add chilli powder and haldi and fry for 2 or 3 more minutes. Use a wooden spatula for stirring regularly and do not allow the onions to stick to the pan. If they do stick then add a few drops of water and stir immediately and then remember to stir more regularly.

Chicken Bhuna

Chicken Shora

Chicken Bhuna

1 portion of onion sauce *(see page 40)*
4 chicken breasts *(cut into small pieces)*
1 heaped teaspoon of gharam masala
Optional: Handful of fresh coriander

When onion sauce is quite brown in colour add the chicken pieces. Cook for about 10 minutes and then add the gharam masala. Continue until the chicken is thoroughly cooked. Add the coriander and cook for another minute or two.

Chicken Shora

Make 1 portion of onion sauce but only use 500g of onions instead of 1kg. The remaining ingredients are the same (see page 40).

Cook as for chicken bhuna but after adding the coriander turn the heat down and add enough boiling water to completely cover the chicken. Simmer for 5 minutes on a low heat.

Chicken with Vegetable

Instead of using boiling water to make the gravy, vegetables may be added to the chicken.

eg 1. carrots (grate and fry in onion sauce for about 10 minutes before adding the chicken)
    2. spinach puree which is sold in tins or use frozen spinach (fry in onion sauce for about 10 minutes before adding the chicken)
    3. potatoes (diced into approx 1 cm cubes and added at the same time as the chicken)
    4. frozen garden peas (added to chicken when the chicken is half cooked)

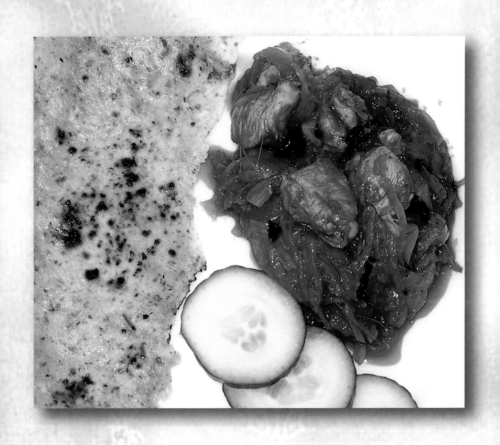

Chicken Karahi

1 kg of onions *(sliced into strips)*
200g of chopped tinned tomatoes
50ml of olive oil or sunflower oil
1 heaped teaspoon of ginger and garlic paste
1 heaped teaspoon of salt
1 heaped teaspoon of red chilli powder
1/4 teaspoon of haldi
1 heaped teaspoon of green chillies *(see spices page)*
1 heaped teaspoon of gharam masala
3 chicken breasts *(cut into small pieces)*
Handful of fresh coriander

Place all ingredients except the gharam masala and chicken into a wok or
a strong saucepan. Fry for about 5 minutes and then add the chicken and
the gharam masala. Fry until chicken is cooked. Add the coriander and fry
for another 2 or 3 minutes.

Prawn Karahi

Replace the chicken in the recipe above with peeled prawns.
As prawns take less time to cook, fry the onions for about 10 minutes
before adding the prawns.

Chicken Korma
Healthy Option if you omit the oil and cream and use extra yoghurt

1 portion of onion sauce with $^1/_2$ teaspoon of haldi and
only 1 teaspoon of red chilli powder *(see page 40)*
1 heaped teaspoon of green chillies *(see spices page)*
2 heaped teaspoons of gharam masala
2 heaped teaspoons of tandoori masala
150g of natural yoghurt *(low fat)*
1 small tub of single cream *(or replace with more natural yoghurt*
for a healthier option)
1 green pepper *(cut into strips)*
3 chicken breasts *(cut into small pieces)*
1 red onion *(sliced into long pieces)*
1 handful of fresh coriander

Place the onion sauce in a strong saucepan or wok. Add the green chillies.
Stir frequently to avoid the sauce sticking to pan (add a few drops of water
if necessary). Fry for 5 minutes until onions are brown. Add the yoghurt and
slowly pour in the cream. Also add the gharam masala at this stage.
Fry for a further 5 minutes. Add the chicken pieces and fry until nearly
cooked. Finally add the pepper, red onion and coriander and fry for
another 5 minutes.

Lamb Bhuna

1 kg of leg of lamb cut into small piece
1 kg onions *(finely chopped)*
200g tin of tomatoes
25ml of olive oil or sunflower oil
1 heaped teaspoon of ginger and garlic paste
2 heaped teaspoons of salt
2 heaped teaspoons of red chilli powder
$1/4$ teaspoon of haldi
1 heaped teaspoon of gharam masala
Handful of fresh coriander

Place all ingredients except the oil, gharam masala and the coriander in a strong saucepan and add 600ml of cold water. Cook using a moderate heat until lamb is tender, stirring occasionally. (If the mixture becomes too dry then add more water.) Add the gharam masala and the oil and fry lamb until the oil separates out. Add the coriander and fry for another minute or two.

Lamb with Vegetable of your choice

See recipe for chicken for choice of vegetables. Cook as lamb bhuna but add the vegetables at the same time as the oil and fry until the vegetables are tender.

Lamb Shora

Use 500g of onions. Continue as for lamb bhuna. After adding the coriander, reduce the heat to a minimum and add enough boiling water to cover the lamb. Simmer for about 5 minutes using a low heat.

Aaloo Keema

Whole Bhindi

Aaloo Keema

500g of minced leg of lamb
750g onions *(finely chopped)*
200g of tinned chopped tomatoes
30ml of olive oil or sunflower oil
1 heaped teaspoon of ginger and garlic paste
2 heaped teaspoons of salt
2 heaped teaspoons of red chilli powder
1/4 teaspoon of haldi
1 heaped teaspoon of gharam masala
2 or 3 potatoes diced into 1 cm cubes
Handful of fresh coriander

Place all ingredients except potatoes, coriander, oil and gharam masala
into a strong saucepan. Using a fairly high temperature, cook until the
mince is almost dry. Add the potatoes, gharam masala and the oil and
reduce to a moderate heat. Place lid over the pot in order to allow the
potatoes to cook in the steam. Stir frequently and do not allow it to stick to
the pan. When potatoes are soft add the coriander and fry for another 2 or
3 minutes.

Keema Mattar

Cook as for aaloo keema but use frozen garden peas instead of potatoes.

Keema Bhindi

Cook as for aaloo keema but use okra (lady fingers) instead of potatoes.
Wash okra before chopping off the top and tail. Discard these and cut the
rest of the okra into small pieces.

Aaloo Mattar

Aaloo Gobi

Aaloo Mattar

1 portion of onion sauce *(see page 40)*
500g of potatoes diced into 1cm cubes
500g of garden peas
1 teaspoon of gharam masala
1 handful of coriander

Add peas and potatoes to the onion sauce. Use a moderate heat and cook with the lid on the saucepan. Stir frequently but replace lid each time until the potatoes are cooked. Add the gharam masala and coriander and fry for another 3 or 4 minutes without the lid on the saucepan.

Aaloo Gobi

1 portion of onion sauce *(see page 40)*
500g of potatoes diced into 1 cm cubes
1 small cauliflower cut into florets *(or use frozen florets)*
1 teaspoon of gharam masala
1 handful of coriander

Add cauliflower and potatoes to onion sauce. Use a moderate heat and cook with the lid on the saucepan. Stir frequently but replace lid each time until the vegetables are cooked. Add the gharam masala and coriander and fry for another 3 or 4 minutes without the lid on the saucepan.

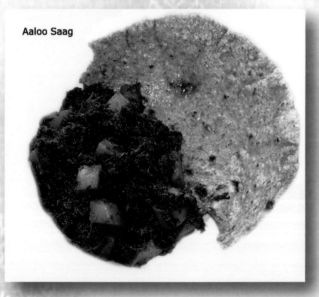

Aaloo Saag

Channa Bhuna

$1/2$ portion of onion sauce *(see page 40)*
800g of boiled chick peas: drain and wash with boiling water
1 teaspoon of gharam masala
1 handful of coriander

Add the chick peas to the onion sauce. Use a moderate heat and fry for 10 minutes stirring frequently. Add the gharam masala and coriander and fry for another 1 or 2 minutes.

Ram Torhi

$1/2$ portion of onion sauce *(see page 40)*
1 kg of courgettes cut into thin slices
1 teaspoon of gharam masala
1 handful of coriander

Add the slices of courgettes to the onion sauce. Use a moderate heat and cook with the lid on the saucepan. Stir frequently but replace lid each time until the vegetables are cooked. Add the gharam masala and coriander and fry for another 3 or 4 minutes without the lid on the saucepan.

Aaloo Saag

1 portion of onion sauce *(omit or use less tomatoes) (see page 40)*
500g of potatoes diced into 1 cm cubes
1 400g tin of spinach puree or use frozen spinach
1 teaspoon of gharam masala
1 handful of coriander

Add spinach to onion sauce and fry for 2 to 3 minutes, then add the potatoes. Use a moderate heat and cook with the lid on the saucepan. Stir frequently but replace lid each time until the potatoes are cooked. Add the gharam masala and coriander and fry for another 3 or 4 minutes without the lid on the saucepan.

Channa Daal

Channa Daal

150g of onions
250g of yellow split peas *(wash until water runs clear and soak overnight)*
200g of tinned tomatoes
50ml of olive oil or sunflower oil
1 heaped teaspoon of ginger and garlic paste
1 heaped teaspoon of salt
1 heaped teaspoon of red chilli powder
1/4 teaspoon of haldi
1 level teaspoon of gharam masala
1 handful of coriander

Make the onion sauce as described on page 40 with the reduced quantities of ingredients. Fry the onions until very soft and the oil has separated out. Drain the yellow split peas and add to the onion sauce. Immediately add 300ml of cold water. Turn the temperature down to a medium heat and allow the daal to simmer for about 30 minutes with the lid of the pot on. Stir regularly and do not allow the water to completely dry - if necessary add more water. Check to see if the daal is soft. Then add the gharam masala and the coriander. Take lid off the pan and leave to simmer on a low heat for a further 5 minutes.

Moong Daal (a yellow pulse)

See ingredients for channa daal but replace the yellow split peas with moong daal.

Wash daal until water runs clear. Soak in fresh water for about 20 minutes. Boil daal for about 10 minutes, drain and add to the onion sauce. Fry on a medium heat until daal is cooked (about 10 minutes).

Add gharam masala and coriander. Take lid off the pan and leave to simmer on a low heat for a further 5 minutes.

Fried Onions
For Curried Eggs

Tarka Daal

250g lentils *(wash until water runs clear)*
300ml of olive oil or sunflower oil
1 heaped teaspoon ginger and garlic paste
1 heaped teaspoon of salt
1 heaped teaspoon of red chilli powder
1 heaped teaspoon of gharam masala
1 handful of fresh coriander
1/4 teaspoon of haldi

Place lentils in 600ml of water with chilli powder, salt and haldi and bring to boil. Simmer on a medium heat for approximately 20 minutes until daal is mushy.

In a separate saucepan pour in oil and add ginger and garlic paste, gharam masala and fresh coriander. Fry for 2 or 3 minutes and add the boiled lentils to the oil. Fry for another 5 minutes on a low heat.

Simple Curried Eggs (for 1 person)

2 eggs lightly beaten
1 small onion sliced finely
1/4 teaspoon each of salt, red chilli powder, gharam masala,
haldi and ginger and garlic paste
50ml of olive oil or sunflower oil
A few leaves of fresh coriander

Place onion, salt, ginger and garlic paste and oil in a saucepan and fry until onions are soft. Add chilli powder, gharam masala, haldi and coriander and fry for another minute. (Adjust the spices to suite your own taste.) Add beaten egg and scramble until egg is cooked.

Halva

Gulab Jamun

Halva

100g of semolina
100g of butter or margarine
100g of sugar
600mls of boiled water
Optional: Sliced coconut shell or sultanas *(soak each of these for about 10 minutes)* or blanched almonds

Dissolve sugar in the boiled water. Melt the butter in a pan and brown the semolina in the butter very gently, stirring continuously. When it is golden brown (approx 5 minutes) add the boiling water with sugar and also the almonds, etc.

Stir for about 10 seconds and remove from the heat. Halva is delicious hot although can be eaten when cold.

Gulab Jamun

50g self raising flour *(sifted)*
100g dried milk *(sifted)*
1 egg
2 tablespoons fresh full cream milk
Syrup
300g of sugar
1 litre of water

Melt sugar in water and boil for about 10 minutes to make a thickish syrup. Meanwhile, mix the sifted flour and sifted dried milk and add egg and fresh milk a little at a time. Make into a smooth dough - knead if necessary until very smooth. Make into small rounds and deep fry in medium hot oil. Fry until dark brown but do not allow to brown too quickly. Drain and soak in syrup where they should double in size. Ready to serve hot or can be eaten cold. Hot gulab jamuns are delicious with fresh, vanilla ice cream!

Zardha

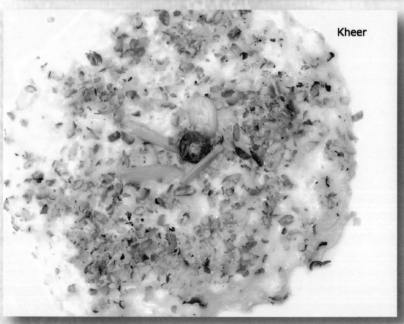

Kheer

Zardha (Sweet Rice)

200g of Basmati rice *(long grain rice)*
Few drops of food colour *(yellow)*
50g of unsalted butter or margarine
150g of sugar
Optional: blanched almonds
Optional: sultanas *(leave to soak for 5 - 10 minutes)*

Wash rice until water runs clear. Dissolve a few drops of food colour in 1 litre of boiling water and add rice. Boil for about 5 minutes and drain. Dissolve sugar in about 1 tablespoon of water, heating gently, and then add butter. As soon as the butter and sugar have melted add the drained rice (and almonds and sultanas).

Stir once or twice very gently and allow all the water to evaporate. Cover the saucepan lid with a tea-towel and place over pot of rice. Reduce heat to as low as possible and leave for about 5 – 10 minutes. Turn zardha in pot before serving.

Kheer (Rice Pudding)

75g of basmati rice
2 litres of full cream milk
150g of sugar
Flaked almonds and grated unsalted pistachio nuts for decoration

Bring milk to the boil and add the rice. Simmer on a very gentle heat for approximately 1 hour. It is very important to stir very regularly to avoid the milk and rice burning at the bottom of the pan. Even if there is only a little bit burnt it will make the taste unpleasant so make sure you use a good pan as well as stirring well. The mixture should now be quite thick so add the sugar and now stir continuously for another 5 minutes. Stir occasionally while the kheer is cooling to avoid a skin forming on the top. Decorate and

Doodh Savaiyang

Savaiyang Bhuna

Doodh Savaiyang (Milky Vermicelli)

100g of vermicelli
1 litre of full cream milk
100g of sugar

Bring milk to the boil and allow it to simmer for a minute. Roughly crumble in the balls of vermicelli and simmer for 1 to 2 minutes, stirring continuously. Remove from heat and leave for at least 5 minutes as the vermicelli will continue to soften with the heat of the milk. Serve hot or when cold, place in fridge. Serve straight from the fridge.

Savaiyang Bhuna (Roasted Vermicelli)

100g of vermicelli
50g of sugar
50g of unsalted butter or margarine

Melt the butter in a pan and crumble the balls of vermicelli into the butter. Brown the vermicelli slowly making sure it does not burn. Use a low heat and stir continuously. When ready add 300ml of boiling water and immediately stir in the sugar. Simmer on a gentle heat until all of the water has been absorbed making sure to stir regularly. Serve hot or cold.

Chuppatti Healthy Option when left unbuttered

400g of plain wholemeal flour
Cold water
Optional: butter

Place flour in mixing bowl and add water a little at a time to make a firm dough. Knead. Leave for about 10 minutes. Knead again and leave for a further 5 minutes. Dough can be made up in advance but do not let it soften too much as it will then be difficult to manage. If necessary refrigerate and remove 5 minutes before use.

Divide into 8 pieces and make smooth balls slightly smaller than tennis balls (approx 3/4 the size). Flatten each ball and roll in dry flour to prevent sticking. Roll out into 8 inch or 20 cm rounds (avoid using any more dry flour if possible). Heat side 1 on a hot griddle or in a strong frying pan for about 15 seconds. Turn over to side 2 and heat until it starts to brown a little. Place side 2 under a hot grill (chuppatti should puff slightly). Then turn chuppatti over to side 1 and place under grill. Chuppatti should now puff up completely. (Don't worry if it does not puff up completely, just grill until cooked.)

Butter the chuppatti on side 1. Fold in half or put one on top of the other with butter sides together.

Wrap chuppattis in a tea towel until all are cooked so that they stay soft.

Any left over chuppattis can be frozen in freezer bags while still warm. Wrap in kitchen roll and warm for about 1 minute in the microwave immediately before eating.

Daal Roti

Mix flour as described in recipe for chuppattis but add tarka daal that may be left over. The amount of water required should be less. You will find that daal roti does not puff up as much as plain chuppattis.

Stuffed Pirrattha

400g of plain wholemeal flour
cold water
Filling of your choice *(Left over aaloo gobi or aaloo peas or make mixture as described in recipe for aaloo tikka or simply use margarine for plain pirrattha)*

Make dough as for chuppattis. Divide dough into 12 and make smooth ball shapes. 2 of these are used to make 1 pirrattha. Roll out 2 of the balls of dough into approximately 4 inch or 10cm rounds. Place filling on 1 of the rounds but not too close to the edge. Then place the 2nd round on top of the filling. Press gently round the edges to seal in the filling. Sprinkle more dry flour on both sides to avoid sticking and roll out the "sandwiched" rounds until you have an 8 inch or 20cm round. Roll gently so the filling does not get squeezed out. Heat side 1 on a medium hot griddle or in a strong frying pan for about 1 minute. Carefully turn over to side 2 and heat for about 30 seconds. While side 2 is being heated butter side 1. Turn over and now butter side 2. Keep turning until both sides are nice and crispy. Place pirrattha in kitchen roll while cooking the remaining dough.

Naan Bread
Healthy Option when left unbuttered and omit the oil

500g of strong plain flour *(white or brown)*
1 packet of easy-blend dried yeast
2 tablespoonfuls of sunflower oil
2 heaped teaspoons of natural yoghurt
Optional: 1 teaspoon of mixed herbs
Optional: butter

Sift flour and add all other ingredients. Mix into a firm dough using warm water. Knead dough for about a minute and then leave in a warm place for about an hour to double in size. Knead again and leave for about 5 minutes.

Divide into about 8 pieces and make a smooth ball with each piece. Roll each ball in dry flour to avoid sticking. Roll out into 8 inch or 20 cm rounds. Heat one side on a medium hot griddle for about a minute. Place second side under a hot grill and allow naan to puff. Butter the naan on side 1. Fold in half or put one on top of the other with butter sides together.

Wrap naans in a tea towel until all are cooked so that they stay soft.

Any left over naans can be frozen in freezer bags while still warm. Wrap in kitchen roll and warm for about 1 minute in the microwave immediately before eating.

Raita

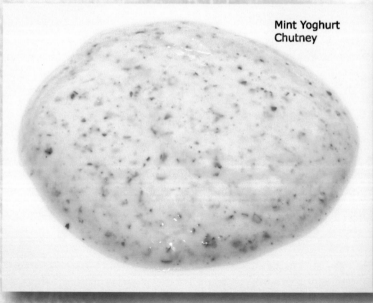

Mint Yoghurt Chutney

Raita
Healthy Option when using low fat yoghurt

450g of natural yoghurt
1/4 teaspoon of red chilli powder
1 level teaspoon salt
1 level teaspoon gharam masala
1 small onion finely chopped
1 tomato finely chopped
10cm piece of cucumber finely chopped

Mix all ingredients. Serve with any starters or may be served with rice.

Mint Yoghurt Chutney
Healthy Option when using low fat yoghurt

450g of natural yoghurt
1 level teaspoon of green chillies *(see spices page)*
1 heaped teaspoon of mint sauce
1/4 teaspoon of red chilli powder
1 level teaspoon salt

Mix all ingredients. Serve with any starters or may be served with rice.

Yoghurt Bhoondi

Aaloo Imlee Chutney Healthy Option

1 teaspoon of tamarind paste
1 carrot grated
1 teaspoon green chillies *(see spices page)*
$1/4$ teaspoon of red chilli powder
$1/2$ teaspoon salt
1 teaspoon sugar
600ml of boiling water

Dissolve the tamarind paste in the boiling water. Add the remaining
ingredients and simmer for a further 10 minutes. Leave to cool.
Serve with pakora, samosas, etc.

Yoghurt Bhoondi
Healthy Option when using low fat yoghurt

450g of natural yoghurt
1 level teaspoon of red chilli powder
1 level teaspoon salt
1 level teaspoon gharam masala and a little more to sprinkle on top
2 heaped tablespoons of bhoondi *(small balls of pastry bought ready made)*

Soak the bhoondi in boiling water for 10 minutes. Drain completely.
Mix all the other ingredients together and then stir in the drained bhoondi.
Sprinkle with the remaining gharam masala. Serve with rice or with
any starter.